W9-CEK-224

JOURNEY INTO CIVILIZATION

ANCIENT EGYPT

by Robert Nicholson and Claire Watts

CHELSEA JUNIORS
A division of Chelsea House Publishers
New York • Philadelphia

Editorial Consultant: George Hart M. Phil,
Education Department, British Museum

This edition published 1994 by Chelsea House Publishers, a division of Main Line Book Co.
1974 Sproul Road, Bromall, PA 19008 by arrangement with Two-Can Publishing Ltd.

First published in Great Britain in 1991 by Two-Can Publishing Ltd., 346 Old Street, London EC1V 9NQ

3 5 7 9 8 6 4

ISBN 0-7910-2704-X
ISBN 0-7910-2728-7 (pbk.)

Printed in Hong Kong by Wing King Tong Co. Ltd.

Photographic credits:
Werner Forman Archive: p5, p17(1), p19(b), p21(b), p22, p24(r), p30(l);
Sonia Halliday: p6; Michael Holford: p1, p6, p10, p11(t), p12, p13, p15,
p16, p19(t), p23, p24(l), p30(r); Ronald Sheridan: p11(l), p17(r), p20, p21(c)

Illustration credits:
Jon Davis (Linden Artists): p4, p8, p11, p13, p15, p16,
p18, p19, p20, p22, p23, p24, p31
Maxine Hamil: cover, pp25-29

Contents

All words that appear in **bold** can be found in the glossary.

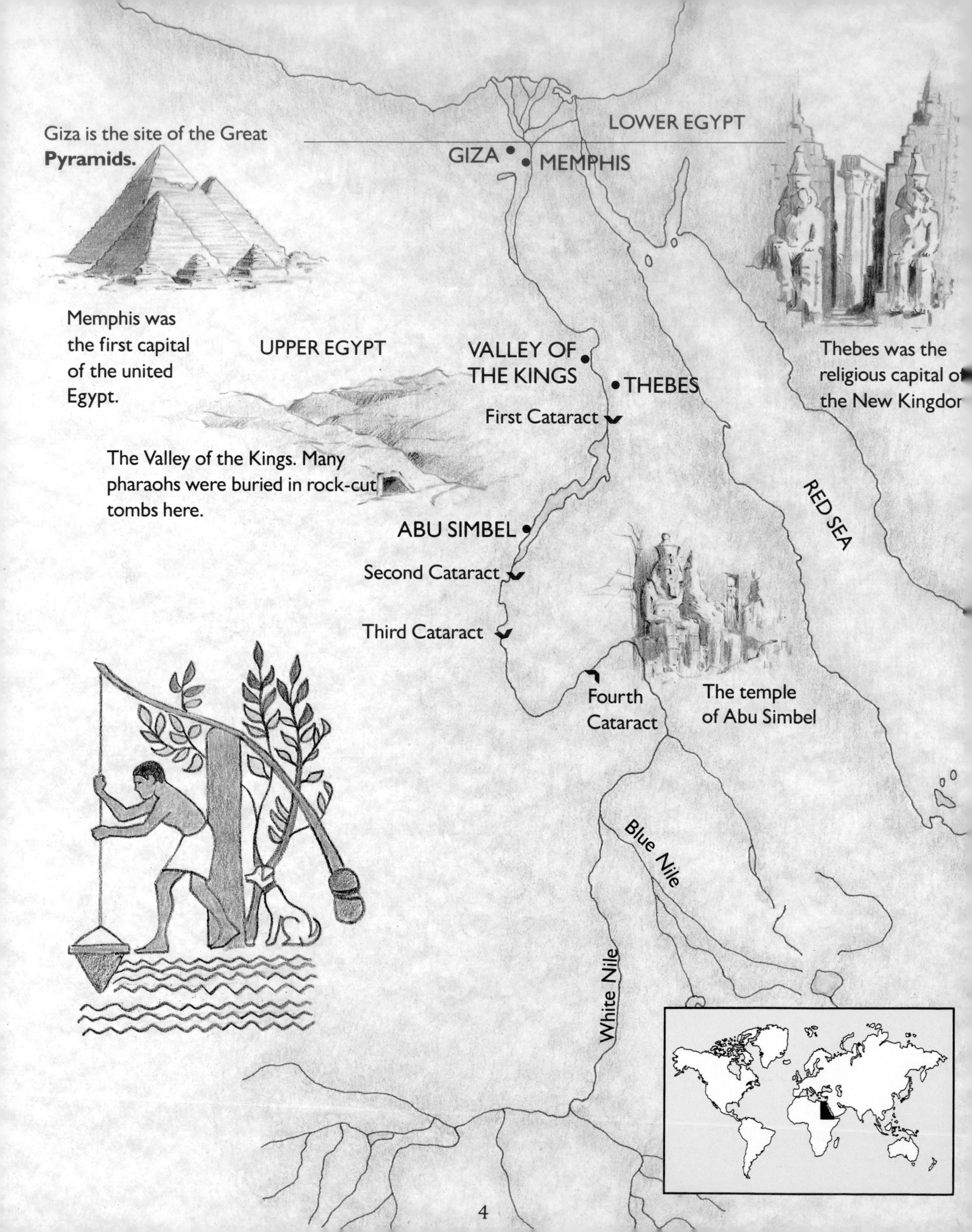
Giza is the site of the Great **Pyramids.**
LOWER EGYPT
GIZA
MEMPHIS
Memphis was the first capital of the united Egypt.
UPPER EGYPT
VALLEY OF THE KINGS
THEBES
Thebes was the religious capital of the New Kingdom
First Cataract
The Valley of the Kings. Many pharaohs were buried in rock-cut tombs here.
RED SEA
ABU SIMBEL
Second Cataract
Third Cataract
Fourth Cataract
The temple of Abu Simbel
Blue Nile
White Nile

The Egyptian World

The great **civilization** of ancient Egypt began over 5,000 years ago, when Menes, the ruler of Upper Egypt, conquered Lower Egypt and united the two kingdoms. The Egyptians never forgot that Egypt had once been two lands, and the **pharaoh** was known as the king of Upper and Lower Egypt.

For the next 3,000 years Egypt remained strong and powerful and gradually expanded to take over new lands. The Egyptians were an advanced people who developed architecture and new efficient methods of government and made important discoveries in medicine and astronomy.

The Gift of the Nile

Egypt is a long, thin country running along the length of the Nile River, an **oasis** surrounded by desert. A Greek arriving in Egypt for the first time called the country *the gift of the Nile*, because it was the Nile that provided most of Egypt's wealth. The rest of Egypt is barren and rocky with little water.

This desert, which the ancient Egyptians called *the Red Land*, cannot support much life, although precious stones and metals are found there. Once a year the **Akhet** or **Inundation** came, flooding the river valley from July to September and leaving behind rich, fertile black mud, *the Black Land*. The amount of water brought by the floods was critical: too little meant that the crops would fail and people would starve, too much and houses, livestock and people would be swept away by the river. For this reason, the water level was constantly measured with a device known as a nilometer, and the changing seasons were carefully monitored to try to prevent famine. To identify the changing seasons, the Egyptians studied the cycle of the sun, the moon and the stars, which led them to divide the year up into 365 days, made up of 12 months each with 30 days and 5 extra days.

◀ The Egyptians also depended on the Nile for transport. They did not usually use carts with wheels, because these were useless in the desert sands or in the mud. Heavy loads were dragged to and from river barges on rollers or sleds.

▼ The green and fertile land around the Nile stands out against the barren desert that surrounds it.

The Pharaoh

The pharaoh of Egypt was an absolute ruler, answerable to no one. Whatever he decided was the law. In fact, another way to say justice was "what the pharaoh loves" and to say wrongdoing was "what the pharaoh hates."

The pharaoh was considered to be a god. He married his own sister or half-sister so that his children would have the blood of the gods. He often had many other wives, too. His subjects treated him with all the honor they gave to their other gods, kneeling before him with their foreheads touching the ground. As a sign of respect they never referred to him by his own name, but used official names instead. One of these was *per-ao*, meaning "great house," which is where our word pharaoh comes from.

A complex administrative system was set up to deal with the governing of the five million people in the empire. The pharaoh's chief adviser, or **vizier,** was the second most powerful man in the kingdom, standing in for the pharaoh and deciding what matters were important enough for the pharaoh's ears. Under the vizier's rule there were numerous local governors called nomarchs who were each in charge of a region or **nome**. They ensured that everyone paid his taxes, which were in the form of goods or services because the Egyptians did not use money.

▼ With all his different religious and administrative obligations, the pharaoh had very little time to himself.

Famous Pharaohs

In the 3,000 years when Egypt was powerful there were over 300 pharaohs. Some were great warriors and some helped to establish the strong government of Egypt, but we know very little about most of them aside from their names.

Tutankhamen

Tutankhamen was just a boy when he became pharaoh. His reign lasted for only ten years but he restored order to the country after the pharaoh before him, Akenaten, had caused chaos by trying to introduce a new religion. Tutankhamen started building a number of huge temples to honor the god Amun-Re.

Tuthmosis III

Tuthmosis, the greatest of the warrior pharaohs, conquered Palestine and Syria and never lost a battle.

Cleopatra VII

Cleopatra was one of the few women to become pharaoh in her own right. She tried to form a political alliance with the Roman empire, first through **Julius Caesar** and then by marrying **Mark Antony**. She killed herself after a huge military defeat.

Gods and Temples

Religion was a very important part of Egyptian life. The Egyptians believed there were gods to take care of every imaginable event or problem. These gods often took on the shape or part of the shape of a particular animal. For example, Bast, the goddess of joy and love, was usually shown as a cat and Anubis, the god who protected the tombs of the dead, was shown either as a jackal or a man with a jackal's head.

Each god had a temple where people could come to worship and ask favors. A statue of the god stood in a room at the back of the temple. It was only brought out on feast days and even then the statue itself was kept hidden inside a shrine. Ordinary people could only go as far as the entrance hall of the temple, where they would meet the god's servant, the priest. The priest would take messages and offerings from the people and tell them the god's answers. Often the animals associated with the god were kept in the temple.

The temple was considered to be the home of the god. Each day meals were laid before his or her statue. Later the food was removed and eaten by the priests.

▼ The temple of Amun at Karnak was extended by pharaoh after pharaoh until it was the size of six huge cathedrals.

Important Gods

RE was the sun god. He took on different shapes at different times of the day.
AMUN was the god of the air and of Thebes. His name means *hidden*. When Thebes became the capital of Egypt, he merged with Re to become the chief god, Amun-Re.
OSIRIS was the god of the dead, who judged all people when they died.
ISIS was the sister-wife of Osiris and the goddess and protector of women.

▶ This wall painting shows Hathor, goddess of music and love, in the form of a cow.

▲ The Jackal was sacred to Anubis, god of the dead.

The Afterlife

The Egyptians believed firmly that with proper preparation a person could live again after death. This preparation involved preserving the body of the dead person and providing it with all the food, furniture, tools and riches it would need in the afterlife. Even the poorest people were buried with scraps of food.

Journey to the Afterlife

Dead persons had to make a long and hazardous journey before they could enjoy the pleasures of the afterlife. They had to pass a giant serpent and a crocodile, avoid being caught in fishing nets and a fiery furnace, and escape from people trying to drown them and chop their head off.

When dead persons reached the underworld, the god Anubis measured their heart against the Feather of Truth. If they balanced, they would be greeted by Osiris, but if not, they would be eaten by a monster which was part crocodile, part lion and part hippopotamus.

▼ In this painting, Anubis weighs the heart of the dead person, while Osiris waits to greet him. Thoth, god of wisdom, records what is happening. Who do you think is the dead person? Can you find the eleven judges?

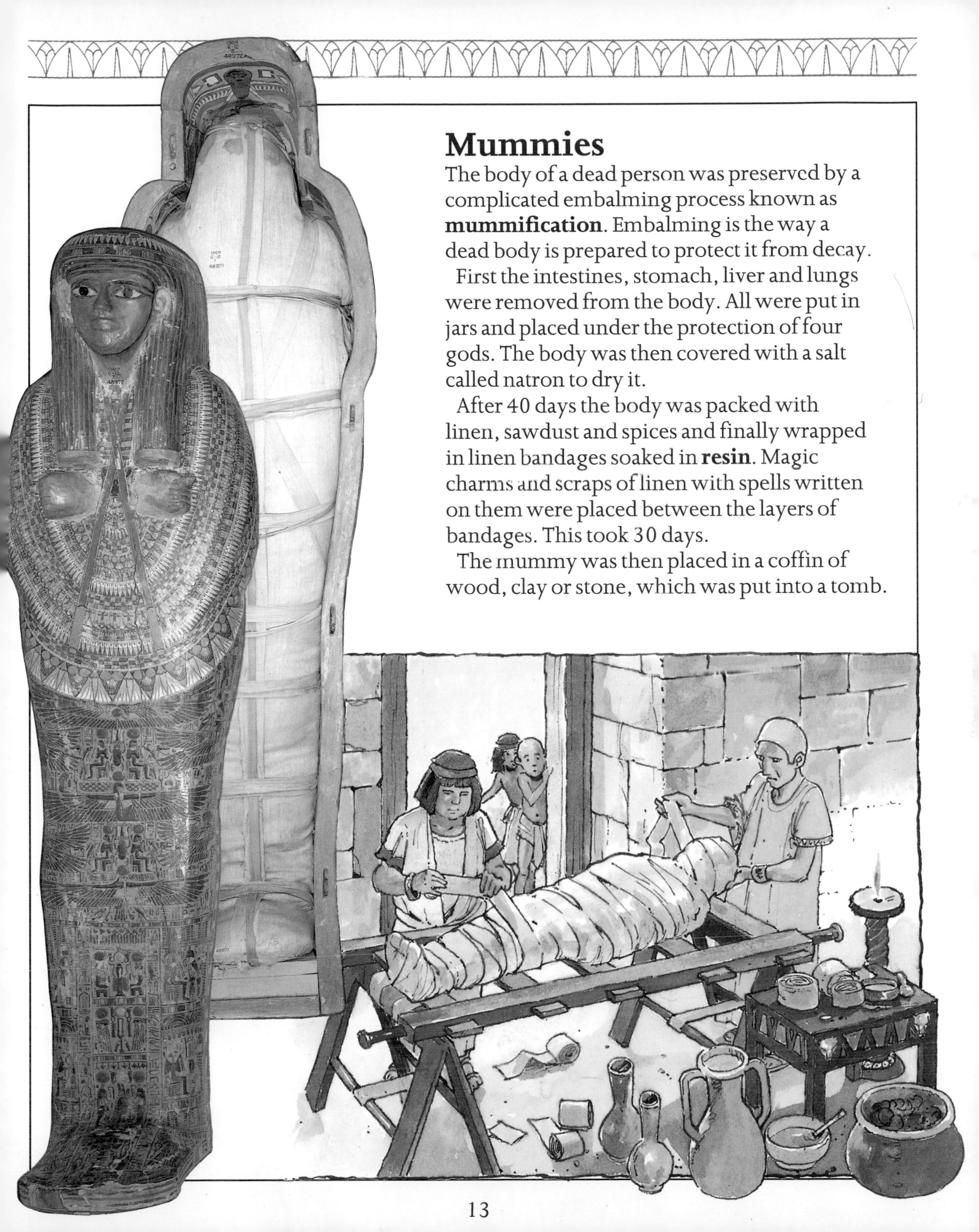

Mummies

The body of a dead person was preserved by a complicated embalming process known as **mummification**. Embalming is the way a dead body is prepared to protect it from decay.

First the intestines, stomach, liver and lungs were removed from the body. All were put in jars and placed under the protection of four gods. The body was then covered with a salt called natron to dry it.

After 40 days the body was packed with linen, sawdust and spices and finally wrapped in linen bandages soaked in **resin**. Magic charms and scraps of linen with spells written on them were placed between the layers of bandages. This took 30 days.

The mummy was then placed in a coffin of wood, clay or stone, which was put into a tomb.

The Pyramids

The tombs of the pharaohs were huge and elaborate and took many years to build. The pyramids were the tombs of some of the early pharaohs. There were so many riches inside that tomb robbing became very common. To prevent this, pharaohs had maze-like tombs hidden underground, but most of these were eventually discovered by tomb robbers anyway.

▼ Ramps of packed earth were built to move the stone blocks to the level where they were needed. Then the blocks were hauled up the ramp and put into place by hand.

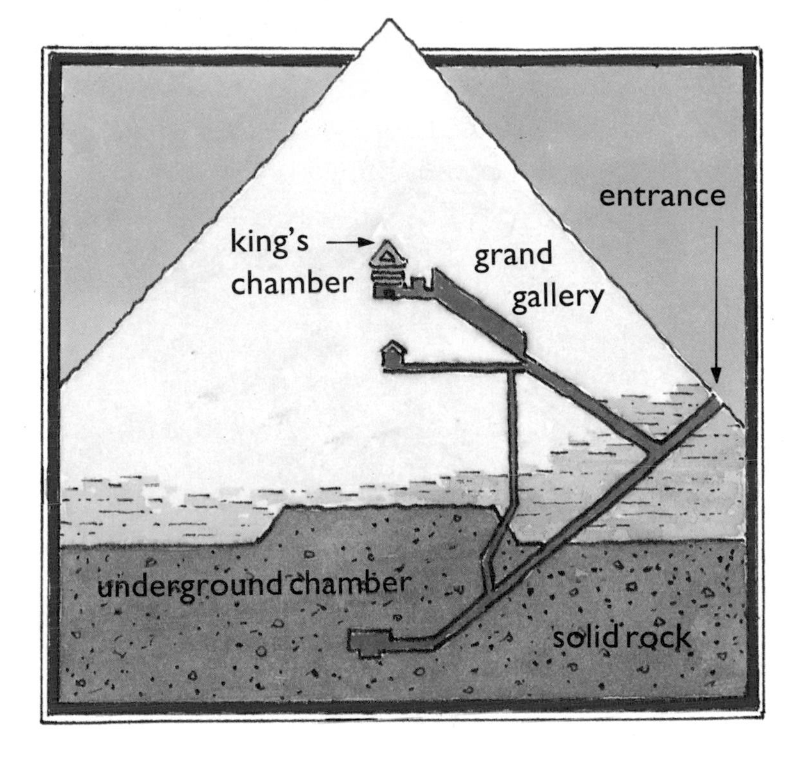

▲ Inside the Great Pyramid.

▼ The Great Pyramid at Giza was originally 482 feet tall. It contained over two million blocks of stone, each weighing about 2.5 tons, although some of them weighed up to 14 tons. It was covered in highly polished limestone which gleamed in the sun. It took 50,000 people 20 years to build.

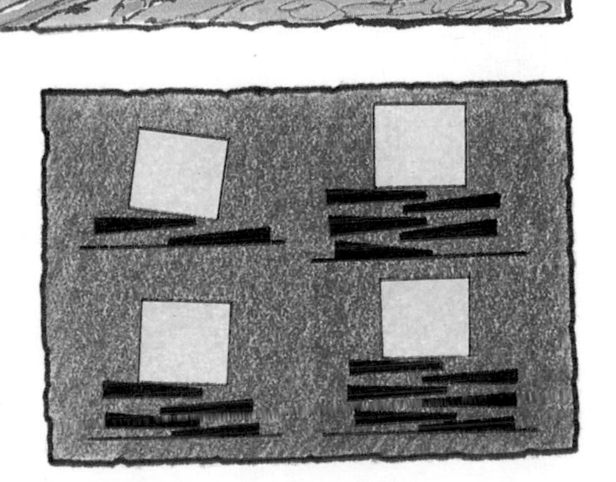

▲ Large blocks of stone could be lifted using wooden wedges.

Writing and Education

Early Egyptians wrote using picture letters called **hieroglyphs**. There were over 700 of these letters, some of which stood for whole words. The word signs were simple pictures illustrating an object or action. For example, a series of wavy lines were drawn to mean water. Other symbols stood for one or two letters. There were no vowels in the alphabet, but the Egyptians managed very well without them. Try writing in English with no vowels — you will probably be able to read it easily.

Gradually hieroglyphs became less detailed to make them quicker and easier to write. This form of writing was used by **scribes** for everyday documents, such as records of taxes. Hieroglyphs were also used for writing on tombs and monuments.

The Egyptians did not use paper but wrote on papyrus, made from reed stems which had been flattened, dried and stuck together to make pages. A thin, sharpened reed dipped in ink was used to write with.

▲ Many paintings in tombs include hieroglyphs which explain what is happening in the picture.

Learning

Most people could not read or write. Children were usually taught a trade or craft by their parents. There were some schools where boys training to be scribes were taught writing, mathematics and astronomy. They learned to read and write by copying and chanting *wisdom texts*, which gave advice on morals and behavior. These schools could not have been very pleasant places to be, because the children were regularly beaten there. One scribe wrote "the ears of a boy are in his back. He listens only when he is beaten."

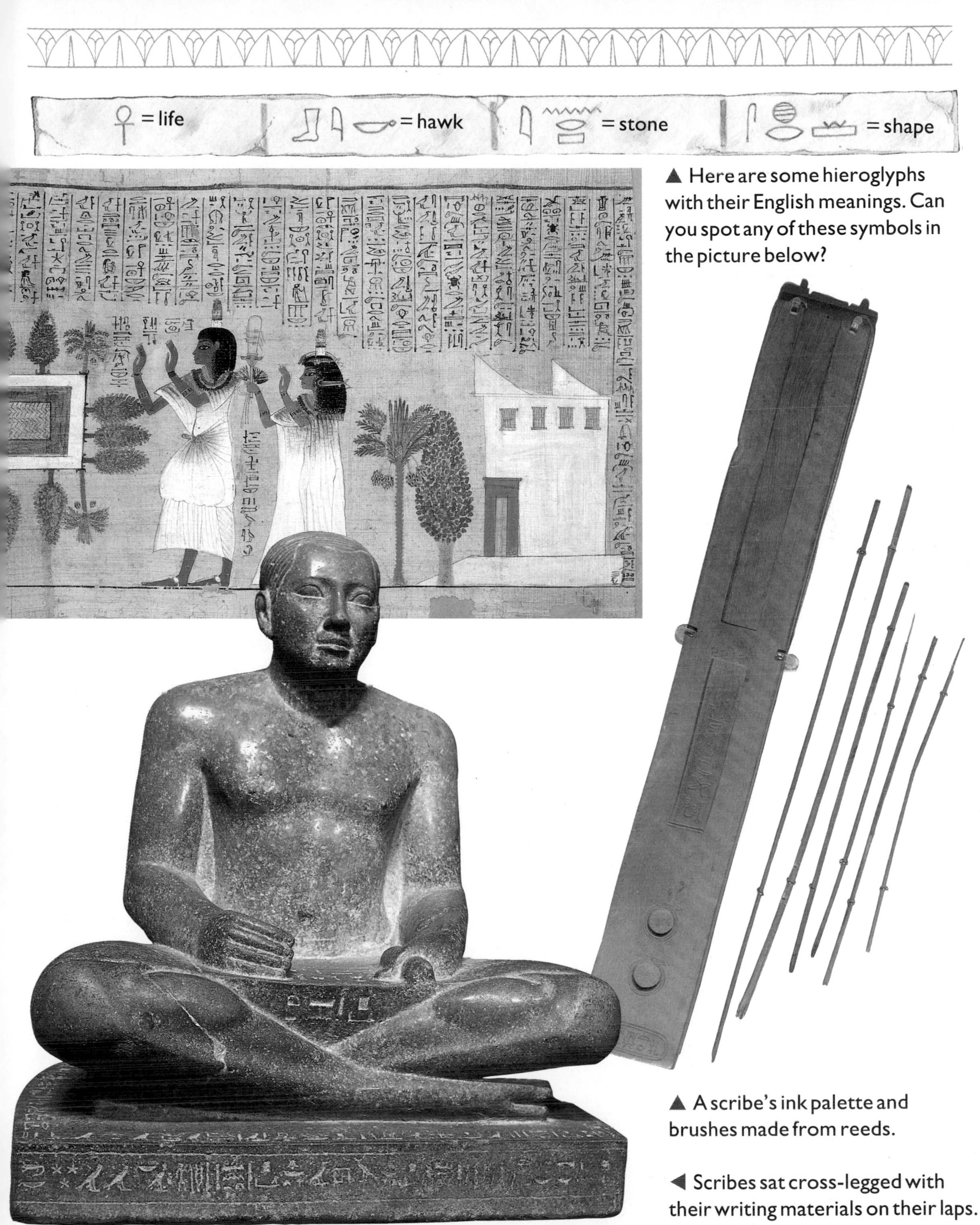

▲ Here are some hieroglyphs with their English meanings. Can you spot any of these symbols in the picture below?

▲ A scribe's ink palette and brushes made from reeds.

◀ Scribes sat cross-legged with their writing materials on their laps.

At Home

Egyptian houses were clustered together on the higher ground at the edge of the river's flood area. They were built of sun-baked brick made from mud and straw. In Egypt's hot, dry climate these bricks lasted a long time. Only buildings that were expected to last for eternity, like temples and tombs, were built of stone.

Houses were very plain, square buildings. They were often surrounded by a wall and had steps outside leading to a flat roof. Inside, the house was dark because of the tiny windows.

The front room of an ordinary house was used by the man of the family to conduct his trade. Sometimes people even kept livestock in this room. There was little furniture in the houses of ordinary people, just a chest for clothes, and storage jars for food.

The second room was usually large with windows high up in the walls. This was used for receiving guests and eating meals. The kitchen, bathroom and bedrooms were at the back of the house.

Sometimes cooking was done on the flat roofs of the houses to avoid the risk of fire.

The houses of the rich looked similar to ordinary houses from the outside, although they were larger. Inside they were decorated with wall paintings and panelling. These decorations could not be displayed on the outside of the house because of the damaging desert winds.

Furniture Facts

● The Egyptians used little furniture. Poor people usually had none, and even the rich often sat on the floor.

● Much of the furniture was portable, like this folding wooden stool (right), which would have had a leather seat.

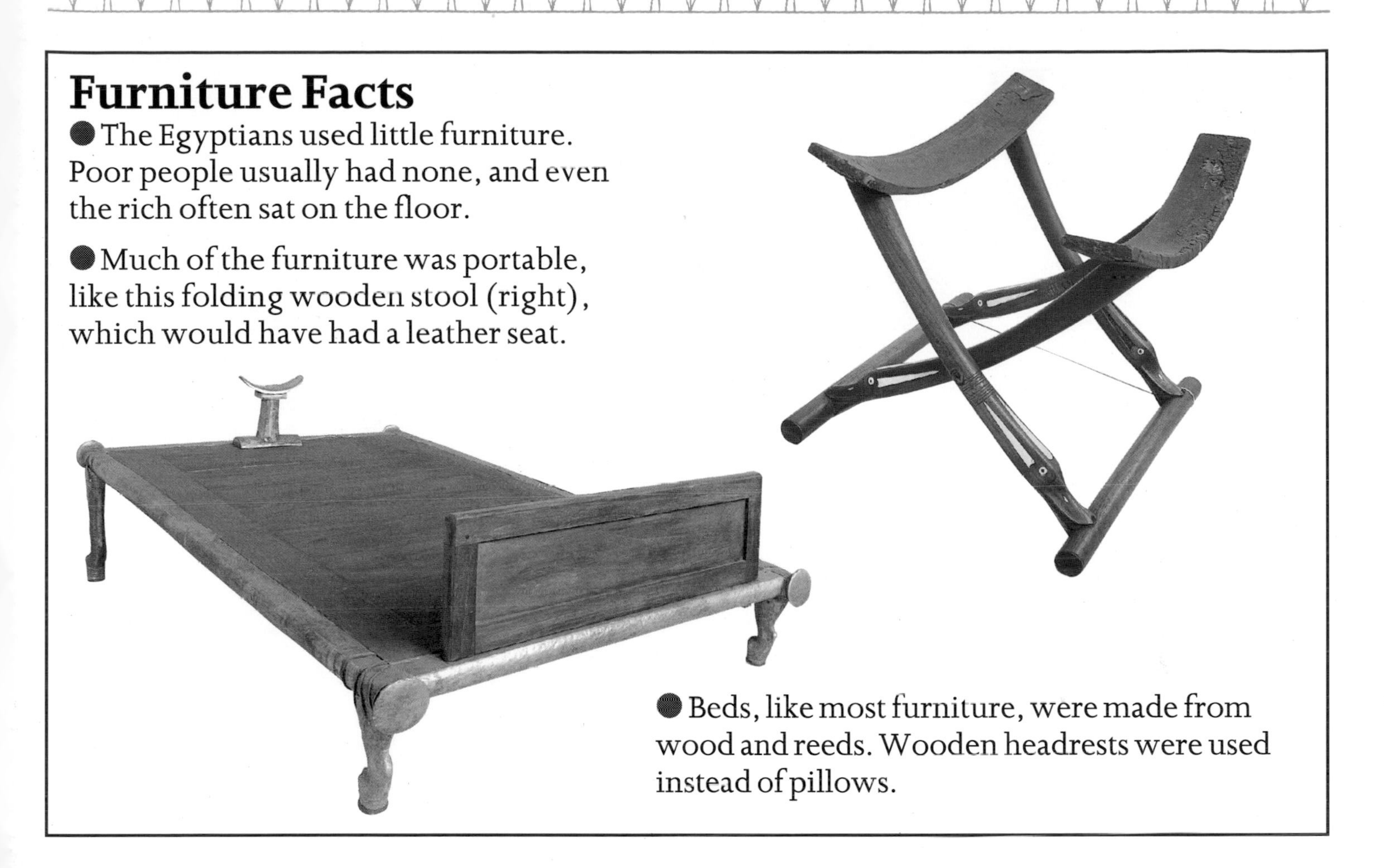

● Beds, like most furniture, were made from wood and reeds. Wooden headrests were used instead of pillows.

Work and Play

Work

Most Egyptians were farmers but some had other jobs. As well as priests, scribes and government officials, there were all sorts of craftsmen. Building projects like the pyramids required hundreds of skilled men: draftsmen to design the structure, masons to carve the stone, painters to decorate the walls, sculptors to carve the statues and other craftsmen to make all the furniture, jewelry, tools and utensils that were to be put inside.

Because the Egyptians did not use money, the craftsmen were paid with food, drink, clothes and lodging. Sometimes the men working on royal tombs went on strike if their payment did not arrive.

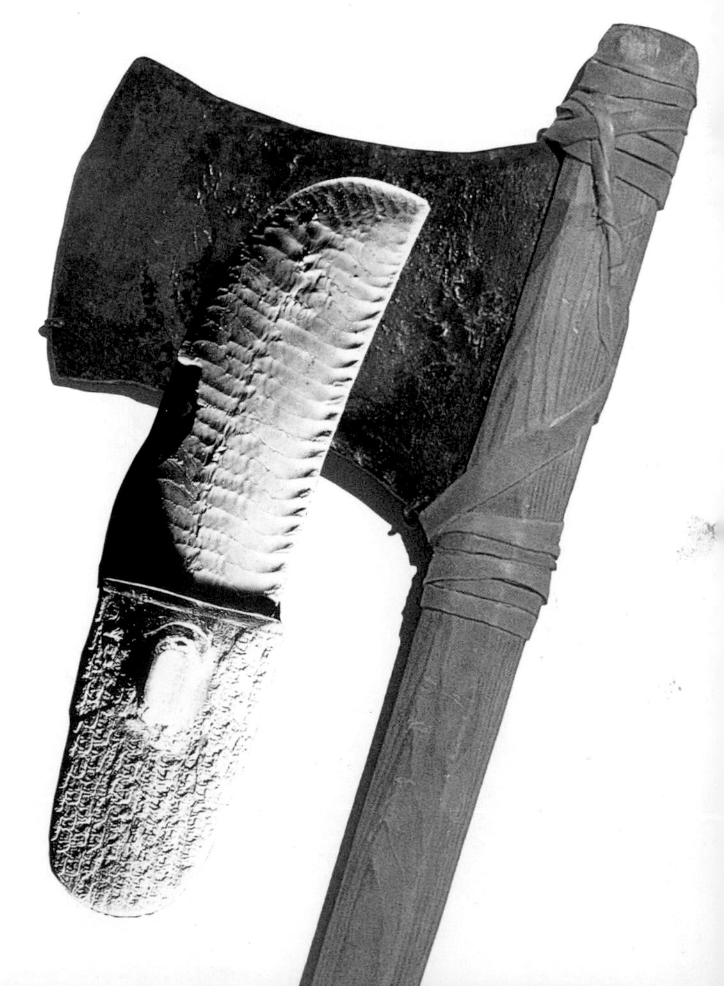

▶ Egyptian craftsmen used tools made from wood, as well as bronze and other metals.

Play

Egyptians worked very hard—sometimes for eight days in a row, followed by two days off. They spent much of their spare time hunting, dancing, wrestling, playing in ball games and performing acrobatics. Rich people held lavish dinner parties, where guests were entertained by acrobatics and musicians.

Board games were also popular and senet was the favorite. It was played on a board divided into three rows of ten squares. Each player had seven pieces and the object was to get all your pieces to the end of the board, while preventing your opponent from doing the same.

Children played with wooden balls and tops as well as dolls and carved wooden animals.

▲ Some Egyptian toys had moving parts. This cat's jaw is operated with a string, and the wooden horse moves along on its wheels.

▶ This senet board has a little drawer to keep the pieces in when they are not being used.

▼ Do you know what games these children are playing?

Food

The fertile soil around the Nile helped produce a wide variety of crops for the Egyptian people. There was a plentiful supply of wheat and barley for bread and beer. Vegetables such as onions, leeks, lettuce and all kinds of beans were eaten in great quantities. They were often served with an oil and vinegar dressing, a lot like modern salad dressing. There wasn't much fruit because it was hard to grow in the extremes of the Egyptian climate. However, the Egyptians did manage to grow figs, dates and pomegranates, and grapes that they used to make wine.

People did not eat a great deal of meat. Cattle were more often kept as beasts of burden and for milk than for meat. Feasts for the rich did include a wide variety of meats, though, including such strange delicacies as antelope and hyena. Fish was eaten mostly by the poor.

When the Egyptians ate they sat on the floor next to low tables. They used their fingers to eat with. The pharaoh had a servant to wash his hands between each course.

Egyptian Bread

Try making your own Egyptian bread with some help from a grown-up. You can add chopped dates to the dough if you like.

You will need:

1 ¾ cups whole wheat flour
225 ml water
½ tsp salt

- Put the flour and salt in a very large bowl.
- Add the water very slowly, mixing well.
- Knead the dough.
- Shape into small rounds or triangles.
- Cover with a cloth and leave overnight.
- Place on a greased or non-stick cookie sheet and bake for 30 minutes at 350°F, or until golden brown.

Mix up the ingredients.

Knead the dough.

Cover the dough overnight before placing on a cookie sheet to cook.

Farming Facts

- There were three seasons in the farming year: the Inundation (June-October), the Emergence (November-January) when the floodwaters subsided, and the Drought (February-June).
- Each farmer's land was marked by heavy stones which could not be moved by the floods.
- A complex **irrigation** system allowed flood water to be stored in huge reservoirs so that it could be used when needed.
- During the Inundation, when little farmwork could be done, many people worked on the pharaoh's building projects as a way of paying their taxes.

▲ Egyptian farmers used wooden plows drawn by oxen.

Clothes

The clothes worn by most Egyptian people were made from linen. Flax, which linen is made from, grows well in the Egyptian climate, and the fabric is cool and comfortable. Most people wore undyed linen, decorated by pleating. Only the rich could afford brightly colored cloth.

Men wore a piece of linen wrapped around their waists like a kilt or a simple tunic. Laborers usually wore linen loincloths or nothing at all. Men were usually clean-shaven or had small, pointed beards.

Women wore ankle-length dresses, often with one or both shoulders bare.

Most children wore no clothes and had their heads shaved, except for a long braid on the right side of their head which was called *the lock of youth*. In cold weather everyone except the priests wore cloaks of wool or animal skins. Sandals were made from reeds or leather, with a strap over the instep and between the first and second toes.

▲ Egyptian mirrors were made of bronze, and combs were made of ivory or wood.

Egyptian Cosmetics

- Personal appearance was very important to the Egyptians. They used perfumed oils to keep their skin healthy in the harsh desert winds.
- Rich Egyptian men and women wore wigs made from a mixture of real hair and vegetable fibers. The strands were attached to a netting base with wax.
- Men and women wore eye make-up to protect their eyes from sand and dust.
- At dinner parties guests and servants wore cones of perfumed oil on their heads. The perfume gradually melted and ran down their hair and clothes.

Nut's Children

The ancient Egyptians told many myths about their gods and about the world around them. Often these stories would try to explain something that the people did not really understand. Nut's Children tries to explain why the moon changes shape.

In long ago times, Re, the chief of all the gods, still reigned on Earth as a living pharaoh. He lived in a huge palace on the banks of the Nile, and all the people of Egypt came to bow down before him. All his courtiers did exactly what he asked, and he spent his time hunting, playing games and feasting. It was a wonderful life!

However, one day a courtier came to him and told him about a conversation he had overheard. Thoth, god of wisdom and magic, had told the goddess Nut that one day her son would be Pharaoh of Egypt.

Re was furious. How could anyone but he possibly be pharaoh? No one else was worthy of the task, and besides, he had no intention of

ever giving up the throne. He paced back and forth in his chambers, shouting at the top of his voice.

"How dare they suggest such a thing! Why, they are probably plotting to get rid of me at this very moment. But no child of Nut will dethrone me!"

He thought and thought about a way to protect his throne. Eventually, summoning all the magic powers he possessed, he spoke these words: "I lay this curse upon her: No child of Nut will be born on any day or any night of any year."

News traveled quickly among the gods, so Nut soon heard of Re's curse. She was heartbroken. She badly wanted a child, but she knew that Re's magic was very strong. How could she break the curse? The only person who might be able to help her was Thoth, wisest of all gods, so she set off to see him at once.

Thoth loved Nut dearly and, when he saw her tears, he decided to do all he could to help her.

"I cannot lift Re's curse," he said, "but I may be able to get around it. Just wait here."

Thoth knew that Khonsu, the moon god, was a great gambler, so he went to visit him and challenged him to a game of senet. Khonsu

did not stop to think for a moment. He could not resist a challenge.

"O, Thoth," he said. "You may be the wisest of all the gods, but I am the greatest senet player there has ever been. I have never lost a game. I will certainly play you and I will win every game easily!"

The two sat down to play. From the very start, Thoth won every game. All seven of his pieces seemed to reach the far end of the board before Khonsu's pieces had even moved.

"You have just been lucky until now, Thoth," said Khonsu. "I bet an hour of my light that I will win the next game."

But still he lost! Thoth kept on winning and Khonsu kept on betting his own light until Thoth had won enough of Khonsu's light to equal five whole days. Then Thoth stood up, thanked Khonsu for the game and left, taking Khonsu's light with him.

"What a coward," muttered Khonsu to himself. "My luck was just starting to change. I would certainly have won the next game!"

Thoth fitted the five extra days in between the end of that year and the beginning of the next. At that time a year was made up of twelve months, each with 30 days, making a total of 360 days in the year.

Nut was overjoyed when Thoth told her what he had done. Because the five extra days

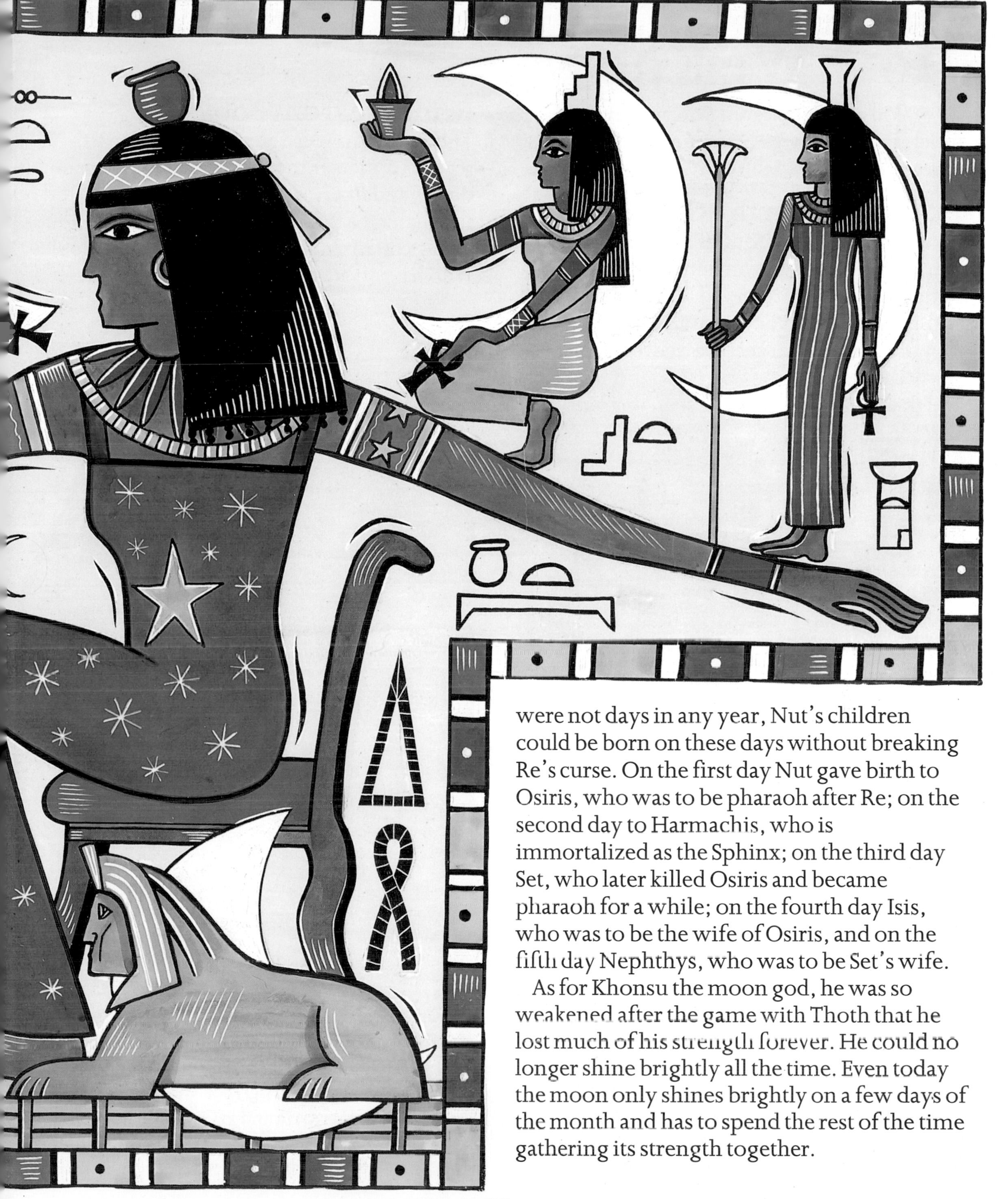

were not days in any year, Nut's children could be born on these days without breaking Re's curse. On the first day Nut gave birth to Osiris, who was to be pharaoh after Re; on the second day to Harmachis, who is immortalized as the Sphinx; on the third day Set, who later killed Osiris and became pharaoh for a while; on the fourth day Isis, who was to be the wife of Osiris, and on the fifth day Nephthys, who was to be Set's wife.

As for Khonsu the moon god, he was so weakened after the game with Thoth that he lost much of his strength forever. He could no longer shine brightly all the time. Even today the moon only shines brightly on a few days of the month and has to spend the rest of the time gathering its strength together.

How We Know

Have you ever wondered how we know so much about the lives of the ancient Egyptians, although they lived thousands of years ago?

Evidence from the Ground

Archaeologists have found many objects which were thrown away by ancient Egyptians and which have been preserved by the hot, dry climate of Egypt. They have also pieced together a very clear picture of everyday Egyptian life from the objects found in tombs and the paintings they have seen on tomb walls.

▲ Tomb-paintings like this one give a detailed picture of life in ancient Egypt.

Evidence Around Us

Many people in Egypt today have a lifestyle similar to that of the ancient Egyptians of thousands of years ago. Farmers on the banks of the Nile still live in houses of sunbaked brick, built in the same style as the ancient houses, and certain farming methods are still the same. A huge dam built on the Nile now controls the flooding of the river and makes people's lives much easier.

Evidence from Books

The Egyptians were great writers. Scribes recorded everything that happened in minute detail, and many of these records survive today. It is thanks to them that we know more about the Egyptians than we do about many peoples who have lived since them.

▲ It was not until 1822, sometime after the **Rosetta Stone** had been discovered, that Egyptian texts could be read. The stone contains writing in hieroglyphs, in an Egyptian script called **demotic** and in Greek. This and other tablets were used to find the key to hieroglyphs.

Glossary

Akhet
The yearly flooding season on the Nile. (Egyptian word)

Caesar, Julius
Roman general who became leader of the Roman empire.

civilization
An organized society which has developed social customs, government, technology and the arts.

demotic
A form of ancient Egyptian writing that was developed from 700 BC onward and was used for business and administration.

hieroglyph
A symbol standing for a word or group of letters used in ancient Egyptian writing.

Inundation
The yearly flooding of the Nile valley.

irrigation
A way to artificially supply water to dry land, usually through a system of channels.

Mark Antony
Roman general who married Cleopatra.

mummification
A process of drying and embalming by which a body was preserved.

nome
What the Egyptians called a province.

oasis
A fertile area in a very dry place.

pharaoh
The ruler of ancient Egypt.

pyramid
A tomb with four triangular sides built for the early Egyptian pharaohs.

resin
A waterproof substance secreted by many plants.

Rosetta Stone
A carved stone which gave a major clue to the deciphering of hieroglyphs. It was found by a French officer in 1799.

scribes
Men whose job it was to write down information.

vizier
The chief adviser to the pharaoh. At times there were two of them.

Index